LAYING THE FOUNDATION

Brick by Brick

2ND EDITION

By

KHADIJAH BUTLER

Laying The Foundation Brick by Brick

2ND Edition

Dedication

To my parents, Craig and Sheila, the compass for what I hope to be.
For those reading this who wear your tragedies as armor,
cheers to making your pain productive.

Contents

Introduction   1

CHAPTER 1: Developing a Scholarship Foundation   6
CHAPTER 2: Private Foundation vs. Public Charity   9
CHAPTER 3: Choosing your Board   13
CHAPTER 4: Scholarship Startup and Execution   23
CHAPTER 5: Budgeting – Funding - Bookkeeping....Oh My!   37
CHAPTER 6: Paperwork, Paperwork, Paperwork!   43
CHAPTER 7: Promoting Your Scholarship and Being Found   49
CHAPTER 8: Fundraising   51
CHAPTER 9: Selecting Your Winners   55
CHAPTER 10: Awarding the Scholarship   59
CHAPTER 11: Triumphs and challenges   63

About the Author   73
About the Craig D. Butler Scholarship Foundation   75
Resources & Checklists   77
Laying the Foundation Brick by Brick: The Playlist   81
Sample Board Meeting Agenda   83
Sample Scholarship Application   85
Sample Bylaws   87

Introduction

I did not want to write this book. I never dreamt of being a writer; I was a precocious little girl from Southwest Philly who wanted to be a doctor on career day. My mother said I was a self-taught reader at four years old. She was doing my hair when suddenly, I began reading the commercial. She handed me a book to ensure she wasn't dreaming, and I started reading it to her. At four, and even now, in my adult life, being an author wasn't a path I thought I would venture down, but my love for learning and sharing my knowledge came quickly. It's funny how reading and research would become parallels for me.

Growing up, I've always 'colored outside the lines' and did things most of my friends wouldn't, a little lioness, a risktaker. I still recall my mom's story of how I wanted to go ice skating, and I was determined at an early age that I would either be the first at something or the best at it. I had never been ice skating a day in my life, but our school offered it as a class trip, and I seized the opportunity. As a kid, you don't think of your fears and the what-ifs, how many times you may fall, if you'll get cut, all things that cross your mind as an adult. Your only thoughts are how much fun you will have being with your friends and feeling free from sitting at your desk daily. When I got to the rink, I held the wall initially, but seeing my classmates push themselves to skate a lap or venture to the middle was my first life lesson in surrounding myself with motivating people. I didn't have balance and even fell several times, but eventually, I got the hang of it. I learned so many life lessons that day. One, I didn't need my parents or the wall to hold me up, and I alone could succeed if I conquered my fear, and two, with falling, you pick yourself back up and start over, as with life. I can also reflect on my experiences developing a tenacity that made me into the woman I am today. At age eight, my dad took my sister and me to our dentist appointment, but on our way home, we detoured through the African American Museum and ran into none other than Courtney B. Vance. My dad was a huge fan, but instead of appearing overzealous, he whispered in my ear, "Baby Girl, go ask for his autograph," I walked right up to him with a pen.

After my father's death, I didn't grieve him initially; instead, I was in a state of shock and stayed there for a few months before it hit me that I would never see him again. I knew I needed something that elevated me from grief to mourning. I could hear his voice nudging me to turn my sorrows into a story. Writing became my sense of healing, and I knew it could lead to someone else's survival. I thought pouring into my community by granting scholarships was the chain reaction of memorializing my father's murder.

But it turned into so much more than that. In my pursuit of starting my foundation, I discovered that there were no scholarships offered to African American college-bound students specific to the Philadelphia community that wasn't funded by a corporate sponsor, endowment/trust, or celebrity. I also knew I wanted to be a catalyst for change.

Providing the tools, resources, and access necessary for students to receive an education would ultimately increase their chances of breaking the cycle of poverty.

Providing scholarships to the community is essential for many to earn an education. Very few students have parents with a college savings plan or an academic/athletic scholarship to fall back on, or they don't want to join the millions of Americans in student loan debt, including myself. This book provides a few steps, tools, resources, and what I like to call "je-wels" to get you started.

I genuinely strive to pay it forward, both personally and now, with my foundation. There's probably a reason I couldn't find a ton of literature out there about starting a nonprofit scholarship foundation: it's 'Survival of the Fittest,' as Mobb Deep says. So, if you made it this far, I applaud you, salute you, hell, I'll pull out the HBCU band for anyone who's purchased this book!

Objectives

Here's what I hope you'll gain from reading this book:

- ▸ The differences between a private foundation and a public charity.
- ▸ Choosing your scholarship cause.
- ▸ Mistakes to avoid.
- ▸ Triumphs and challenges.
- ▸ And so much more.

We salute all the scholarship foundations and their effort in granting the gift of education. No matter the cause you are behind, we wish you luck in your new adventure!

Kind Regards,

Khadijah Butler, MS
Founder & President

Chapter 1

Developing a Scholarship Foundation

There are several reasons why people decide to start a scholarship foundation. Some are fundamentally driven to help others; it's in their nature, essence, and being. But if you're familiar with the Craig D. Butler Scholarship Foundation or CDB Scholar-ship your motivation is personal, like mine. My father, Craig D. Butler, was murdered at the hands of a 14-year-old in 1999. My family and I decided to commemorate my father's legacy to live on through the joy and opportunities of education versus the pain and darkness of gun violence.

Whatever your motivation, the first step is *(1) Determine who you're helping and (2) Define your mission.* Perhaps you're a minority fe-male with a disability, or you're a product of the foster care system. Maybe you want to be a part of a cause that's special to you. The point is that there is always someone in need who will benefit from the

Jewel

Set your scholarship foundation apart from other scholarship awards.

problem you are attempting to solve. Everything starts with an idea, but you must develop your foundations' values and the organizational approach after the concept. If the structure of your foundation will be a nonprofit, defining your mission is vital. CDB Scholarships' mission is to provide financial assistance to African Americans pursuing higher education in the aftermath of gun violence. Our cardinal principle is to ensure that African Americans from underserved populations are not economically disadvantaged and receive a quality education. When applying for your 501c3 status, a question on the 1023 form asks for your organization's purpose, so not having it puts you at risk of your application being rejected for tax-exempt status.

One je-wel I want to add is choosing a cause broad enough to be considered a charitable class but unique enough that sets your scholarship foundation apart from other scholarship awards. The idea is to allow the students applying to be eligible and inclusive. CDB Scholarship, for example, offers scholarships to African American high school seniors in Pennsylvania. Our nonprofit is classified as a minority scholarship and a local scholarship. When choosing your cause, check government guidelines to ensure that your scholarship follows all legal requirements and is not discriminatory.

Dive deep

When defining your mission, you must dive deep. Write down basic questions and answers to the purpose of your foundation. A few questions you may ask yourself are:

- Why am I starting a scholarship foundation?
- What is my foundation's mission?
- What geographic area will we serve?
- What cause am I passionate about?
- Who is the target audience that my foundation will serve?
- Who will serve as my board members?
- Will we apply for grants, and if so, what types are we eligible for?
- How will we pay for services and raise funding for our day-to-day operations?

Answering these questions is the first step in expounding your plan of action for your foundation. Ultimately, you want a visual 'yellow brick road' to see the mission from beginning to end.

Chapter 2

Private Foundation

vs.

Public Charity

So you did your deep dive, answered your tough questions, and nailed down your purpose. Great! Now, just eight more to go. Ain't no half-steppin' you gotta be on your Big Daddy Kane. We just getting started!

Now, it's time to choose the type of scholarship foundation that aligns with your organization's structure. There are two primary types of structures: private foundations and public charities. Private foundations usually operate to financially support other public charities rather than directly operate charitable programs.

Some private foundations that come to mind are the Bill and Melinda Gates Foundation, The Nemours Foundation, and the Robert Wood Johnson Foundation. Public charities, on the other hand, are designed solely to operate for direct benefit to the public.

Some of my favorites are UNCF, the American Red Cross, and, of course, the Craig D. Butler Scholarship Foundation!

There are many reasons why some organizations may choose a private foundation vs. public charity:

Private Foundation vs Public Charity

It is not tax-exempt but has tax incentives	Tax-exempt contributions are deductible
Funded by family or corporation; Greater financial control	Funding is dependent on public support and the Board of Directors
Legacy opportunities for your family	The organization belongs to the public.

Private Foundations are typically for the high-earning, those with passive income, and an excellent choice for those who want to create a family legacy. Some individuals utilize this way of giving to give back beyond random donations to charities to make a lasting lifetime impact. Private foundations also provide incredible tax savings; they give you the flexibility to who you can grant money and allow you more significant influence over social change without being overly consumed by the day-to-day management of a public charity. The drawbacks of a private foundation are that they are subject to extensive scrutiny, the paperwork can be complex, and after hiring lawyers, accountants, and investment advisors, those fees add up!

Despite the pros and cons of a private foundation vs. a public charity, I chose the public charity route to connect with the students, the community, and the city council advocating for gun violence. I also wanted to be a part of my students' journey rather than just being a faceless blank check.

Before I chose the public charity route, I had to wrap my head around the concept that I would never own my nonprofit as the organization's founder. Perpetual existence in the flesh!

I had to think of it as a street. You can name and develop the street, but you don't own the street. If you go outside right now and look at the name of the street where you live, the developer of your street likely developed the land and may have even created the name, but he doesn't own the street. The city or the county owns it, and that street will be here long after you.

The point is your vision for philanthropy is more significant than yours. You must be willing to accept the time and resources you're investing in is a selfless act. You must understand that you are building value for future generations when starting your foundation; ultimate stewardship is key!

Chapter 3

Choosing your Board

No matter what structure you choose for your scholarship foundation, choosing your board of directors is vital. If you are a newly formed nonprofit, typically, your board will be small and consist of family, friends, and people you trust. You want to select those who believe in its founder, mission, and foundation's future. You want people who are ten toes down, riders, those who are with you when it's time to work AND when it's time to shine.

Some of the characteristics of a good board member include:

▸ **Enthusiasm:** Is this individual excited about helping your foundation succeed? Do they have a passion for your mission? Do they have a cheerful outlook overall?

▸ **Experience:** Does this individual have experience in your cause?

Perhaps their experience can be rooted in your mission statement, or their expertise could be personal. For example, my sister is a board member who, for obvious reasons, knew my dad personally, but one of my officers has sat on his fraternity's board for their scholarship program.

▸ **Diverse:** Are the individuals selected from diverse backgrounds, ages, etc.?

▸ **Symbiosis:** Are the individuals selected for the board have similar temperaments? Are they level-headed and on the same page when making decisions?

▸ **Attentive:** Will this individual remain alert when there are signs of trouble, or are they asleep at the wheel? Will they jump into action to resolve a problem?

Jewel

Ensure your bylaws are written to reflect the steps needed if a board member resigns.

If you're a founder, you will need to lean on them, pick their brains on things you may not have knowledge of, and provide unique perspectives you alone can't. You want those with an entrepreneurial mindset who are forward thinkers and can take the initiative. These steps are just a start, but the takeaway is cultivating a board that will make your scholarship foundation unstoppable.

If a board member is no longer engaged in the mission and their focus changes, ensure your bylaws are written to take the necessary steps when receiving their resignation, with or without cause. You don't want to hold someone back who no longer serves your foundation's purpose.

Basic Board Structure

Defining the structure of your board will vary depending on which state your foundation is incorporated or the state your foundation is operating. Before you start dubbing yourself a chairperson who sits on a board, slow down like Brand Nubian! 😊 😊 In the State of Pennsylvania, a 501 © (3) nonprofit board must have at least three members who are unrelated and typically hold the positions of president, secretary, and treasurer. One member may be selected to serve in multiple positions. The President, Secretary, and Treasurer are the three most common roles, but this will depend on which state your foundation is incorporated in or which state your foundation is operating. For example, the District of Columbia only requires a minimum of a President and a Treasurer, but in North Dakota, only a President and Secretary are required board members.

The **President** serves at the discretion and under the supervision of the Board as the general manager, the Executive Director, and the leader. They will have the autonomy of running the day-to-day operations of the foundation under the guidelines provided by the board. In most states, they may also serve as the Chief Financial Officer in the absence of a treasurer. Depending on the state, this term is interchangeable. This role can also be named the Chair or Co-Chair. The President is the figurehead of the foundation, the primary point of contact, and the person who pushes the foundation's vision and provides resolve. This person will lead all board meetings and oversee vendors, partner alliances, and board oversight. Essentially, this person has various responsibilities on any day of the week, and it's their job to ensure it's complete.

The **Secretary's** primary responsibility is to maintain the foundation's records, manage and organize the foundation's meetings and agendas, have a general awareness of the foundation's timelines, and keep track of board member terms. They are the gatekeepers; they should be able to tell you where EVERY single document is without hesitation. Typical responsibilities include sending out notices for all meetings, keeping meeting minutes, ensuring the meetings are organized, and ensuring all attendees are prepared.

Let's say the next meeting agenda calls for an upcoming fundraiser, and each officer is responsible for providing feedback on potential venues. The Secretary's role is to ensure that all input is easily accessible when needed. CDB Scholarship's tool to manage our records is One Drive and a good ole fashioned portable filing box. One Drive is incredible because it's searchable and secure, and it allows us to locate a document in a pinch. We also print copies of specific documents and file them in a portable filing box to have a physical copy of a record when requested or if we don't have access to a computer.

For example, let's say you're having computer issues and can't access any of your files, but you're meeting with a donor for potential funding. Yes, you could perform a tax-exempt organization search on the IRS's website, but what if the Wi-Fi is shoddy or there's no internet access in the building where you're meeting your donor? Having a physical copy of critical documents builds credibility and demonstrates thoughtful planning on your foundation's behalf.

Sometimes, a secretary has variations on what their responsibilities are. Depending on the size of the foundation, some secretaries are accountable for signing off on the foundation's records, such as bank documents, charity registration, and Articles of Incorporation. Some secretaries may also be tasked with keeping track of the term lengths of board members and officers. For example, in Pennsylvania, terms for board directors are only one year, but if your board is in South Carolina, Tennessee, or Wyoming, board terms have a five-year maximum.

The **Treasurer** is the go-to for all sums of money received, spent, and donated to the organization. This includes your foundation's bookkeeping and auditing records, use of the company's credit card, managing payment methods, depositing checks received, managing the nonprofit's budget, etc. As your foundation grows, or you begin receiving grants and donations over a certain amount, the treasurer plays a considerable role, and on top of the characteristics mentioned above, they MUST be trustworthy! You want a treasurer like Tyra Banks, someone so frugal her accountants told her to SPEND money! Your foundation is your legacy. The last thing you want to worry about is mismanagement of the foundations' funds or, worse, fraud.

In many states, a treasurer may not be a required role on your board, and if you're still in the startup phase, you may not need one, but if you begin struggling with maintaining all the financial records or if you begin receiving a lot of grants and donations, consider looking into it.

Board Composition

There are a few different rules for structuring your board with a public charity and private foundation:

Private Foundation vs. Public Charity

Restrictions on members being paid	Officers can be paid.
Composed entirely of family members if desired but also a mix of trustees	51% of the board are unrelated by blood or marriage
Large, odd number of officers and directors to vote (9-20)	Small, odd number of board members needed to vote (5-7)
Family members are unified through philanthropy, 'The Glue that ties the family together.'	Nonfamily members unify the community by way of the cause, 'The glue that ties the cause to the community.'

Family and Friends on Nonprofit Board

When you're starting, it's common to have family and friends on your board, especially if your organization is small, for several valid reasons: There's a level of trust with the family that isn't established yet with a volunteer. There's also an opportunity to include younger family members to move the legacy forward. However, what are the risks associated with having family and friends on your board that could be problematic down the line?

Scenario 1: Let's say a husband and wife sit on your board, and they both vote to use a specific venue for a fundraising event. What policies are in place to ensure they are objective about the venue? Is there a formal process established in your bylaws for choosing vendors and voting fairly? For this type of situation, it's best to include three other members on your board who are not family for a total of five board members so decisions are balanced and unbiased. You want your board to think things through carefully when making decisions on behalf of the foundation and not just echoing the views of their family.

Scenario 2: Your strategic plan consists of outreach initiatives for the foundation, which requires each member to find volunteers, donors, and supporters. However, everyone on your board went to high school and college together, and you all live in the same city. This type of overlap in your circle is counterproductive. You want your board to be diverse with different networks who can bring skill sets your circle doesn't have.

Scenario 3: A family member moves away because they're ready to retire. Managing a nonprofit involves a lot, especially if you're a founder, president, or chairperson, and family members' effort and loyalty to the foundation may become short-lived. Begin developing a transition strategy or a succession plan to relieve your family when the time comes. Use the family members' transition as a launchpad for new beginnings. Truly engage your board to begin thinking of what the foundation's next leader will look like.

Ultimately, you want your board to consist of those who care more about the mission than they care about their alliances with you.

Paying Your Board

Paying your board is a dilemma of capacity vs. ability. The IRS says you CAN pay your nonprofit board legally, but are you CAPABLE if you're still struggling with funding the nonprofit? Initially, the idea is for your board to come together to leverage each other's network for the greater good of the cause. But unless you're receiving a salary grant to accomplish this, the question isn't if you can, it's if you should.

There are pros and cons to paying your board, and it depends on what phase your foundation is in:

▸ If your budget is large enough to include salaries or your board members are providing financial support to the foundation, paying your board may keep your members motivated, justify the time and effort they are investing to further the mission, and allow your foundation to attract top talent.

▸ If your budget is barely large enough to manage the foundation's operating costs, paying your board may not align with your donor's intent. Donors expect their funding to be used for the foundation's operations and scholarship awards. How would it look to ask for donations and then turn around and use it to pay your board's salary? In addition, all compensation is documented and included in the foundation's tax filing and made public. Are you or your board members comfortable with their salaries being available to the public?

In the startup phase, you must adopt a mindset that you may be a working board but are setting a path where you won't be forever. At some point, you, as a founder and board, will begin making enough to pay yourself as you grow. When the budget is developed each year, ensure that salaries are written in, even if they start as a small line item in year one and expand in year four. This exercise will get you conditioned to include salaries each year so you're cognizant of how much you need to raise. When you are ready to pay your board during the nonprofit's growth and maturity phases, ensure the compensation details, including the amount and frequency, are outlined in your bylaws. Make sure you're also utilizing multiple income sources besides grants and donations to include in the budget so that salaries are always included in the future.

Chapter 4

Scholarship Startup
and Execution

So, here is where the fun, patience, and heavy lifting begin! Depending on how quickly you want to start your scholarship foundation, you can either begin the startup paperwork in parallel to your other activities or start in tandem. As a disclaimer, consult with an attorney or tax professional if you have any questions on this process. I am not a guru or a licensed expert, and I ain't tryna have y'all out here in these streets blaming me if something goes wrong 😊.

1. Decide on a name for your scholarship.

This only applies if you're starting a scholarship that aligns with your mission and not a memorial scholarship in honor of a loved one. Take your time choosing a name that's memorable and evokes emotion. The name of your scholarship should motivate people to get involved and stay involved. It's also great to incorporate your cause or mission in the name so it's easier for potential students and donors to find your business online.

a) Once you've chosen a name, complete a Google search to see if the name is already in use. The last thing you want to do is compete with another organization for online ranking.

b) Check with your Secretary of State to make sure the name you've chosen is not in use, and if not, register your foundation's name.

2. Hold your first official board meeting.

The first official board meeting is the informal kickoff of your foundation. It's the time when your board should be figuring out your mission and vision, when you should be reviewing and finalizing the bylaws, and when you can decide to vote and approve additional members of your board. It's also the time to think of each member's roles and responsibilities, set calendar dates for future meetings, and record the meeting minutes. Most states will suggest you have an annual meeting at minimum, but as a startup foundation, you should meet more frequently to ensure your board is aligned. Depending on the size of your board and the topics to be discussed, I would recommend meeting quarterly in the first year or two. Ensure you're prepared with an agenda at least a week or two before each meeting.

a) *Note:* Try not to be all rigid and formal, coming up in there with a gavel and a robe on your Judge Judy! The goal is to set a tone of professionalism but establish a dynamic that allows your members to take on an active role. Remember what I mentioned earlier: You don't own the nonprofit, and this initial meeting will give your board a sense of ownership. Stay on course, but allow your board to be seen and heard.

3. Develop your scholarship's strategic plan.

So, this can sound formal and a bit daunting, but it's not trust! Creating a strategic plan can be as straightforward or as detailed as you want to make it as long as you create it! This tool will serve as your foundation's three-to-five-year roadmap, including your list of donors, community partners, staff, and supporters. It should also include all foundation activities, fundraising plans, and your budget. In my case, I'm already a sticky note/checklist kinda woman when an idea comes to mind, but I also collate them into my strategic plan instead of keeping it in my head. This plan will help you realize your vision in the allotted time and can be revisited anytime.

Let's say you want an in-person fundraising event in year two. How will this take place? How often will the board meet to prepare? How much funding will be used? Your strategic plan will serve to keep you on course.

4. Establish your scholarship contact details, including location, website, and email address.

I followed a ton of blogs, eBooks, and articles that suggested establishing business details AFTER I incorporated the structure of my foundation, but what a huge mistake! When I incorporated my foundation, I was still developing my website, which offered a permanent business email address. Since I was doing this in parallel, my Secretary of State account, Articles of Incorporation, and DUNs number were registered under a temporary Gmail address, which I wound up being locked out of because I forgot my password!

a) You will want to secure your permanent business email immediately because it has greater credibility than a Gmail account. If you ever get locked out of a business account, a dedicated customer service line typically assists with restoring your emails. This is critical when applying for your EIN and filing your 990 Form.

b) If you're going to use a P.O. box instead of a physical location, I recommend a location you or your board easily frequent. This is critical when receiving the status of your nonprofit approval from the IRS. I would also recommend using USPS over UPS. They're affordable, offer fantastic discounts, and you can pay quarterly and cancel anytime. UPS is great for larger organizations, brick-and-mortar companies, or organizations that utilize several shipping services; however, UPS is double the rate you pay upfront every year, and closing your P.O. box is non-refundable until your yearly contract is up.

5. Create bylaws.

Your bylaws are a legal guideline that dictates the policies around how your board will operate. This guideline is your go-to, your protocol, your SOP (Standard Operating Procedure for my fellow Pharma folks) in running your foundation day-to-day. This document is necessary when opening your foundation's bank account and required when completing the 501c3 application if you are going the nonprofit route.

Your bylaws are a living document that should be reviewed and updated regularly (at least every two years) and typically are about ten pages long. When drafting your bylaws, consider the policies necessary to your mission, but try not to get too wrapped up in making the first version perfect. Start with your high-level items, such as meetings, elections, your charity's purpose, etc., and then progressively amend them over time.

If you want to Google bylaw templates to get a general idea of how you want to draft your bylaws, go right ahead. However, the document your board will use to submit for your 501c3 status should come from the state you are incorporating. This is important since the terminology is different from state to state. For example, most states require board meetings annually, but Ohio has a specific default date for meetings to be held on the first Monday four months following the close of the fiscal year. Check for sample bylaws from your state's website so your foundation is cooperating legally. If you've paid for a document filing service like SwyftFilings or Legal Zoom to incorporate your business, they'll often include a template.

6. Incorporate your business entity at the Secretary of State's office in the state where your scholarship will operate.

Depending on the type of scholarship foundation you're forming, you can incorporate as a Nonprofit, C Corp, or S Corp. You must file your Articles of Incorporation, complete a Docking Statement, and submit it to the IRS. There will be different filing requirements from state to state, so consult with a legal professional or the state directly for further details.

a) ***Note:*** As a registered nonprofit, a registered agent is required, and this typically is the Director or Officer of the nonprofit, unless you've decided to use document filing services like Swyft Filings or LegalZoom to serve as your registered agent.

A registered agent's primary purpose is to secure a physical address for the foundation to receive all legal documents since using a P. O. Box is prohibited. The registered agent also needs to be located at an address where someone is available during regular business hours. I highly recommend using an address other than your founder's or board member's to protect their privacy and your foundation's reputation. I would also recommend hiring an outside registered agent since they are equipped to oversee your foundation's paperwork, time-sensitive filings, and any other legal matters you may not have a clue how to manage.

7. Apply to the IRS for an Employer Identification Number (EIN).

For those who don't know, an EIN is your unique business identification number, essentially a social security number for businesses. Your EIN is necessary when filing your business taxes, opening your business bank account, and applying for your 501c3 tax-exempt status. You should apply for an EIN once your foundation has been incorporated into the state of your scholarship.

a) *Note:* It would make sense if the person applying for the EIN is the founder, officer, or authorized member since their social security number will be used for the application. Once the EIN is approved, the personal SSN will no longer be used.

b) *2nd Note: DO NOT PAY FOR YOUR EIN!* There are SOOOO many sites out there that charge you for an EIN when the process is free and immediate. If you have your business name, mission, and all pertinent details, I implore you to take five minutes to apply for this on the IRS's website. It's a piece of cake, literally!

c) *3rd and Final Note:* Once you receive your EIN, it's permanent. It's yours, never reused or reassigned, even if you close your foundation. If you receive your EIN after your 501©3 status is approved, it becomes your 501©3 number.

8. Open your foundation's bank account.

Most major banks and credit unions will ask for your EIN, Bylaws, and Articles of Incorporation when opening a business bank account. They will also ask for authorized members signing checks on behalf of the foundation, who will most likely be your primary officers.

Now, depending on the structure of your foundation, most banks may ask for more documentation about whether you have a nonprofit structure vs. an LLC. When I opened my nonprofit account, they wanted Bylaws signed and dated by the Founder and a letter on Company Letterhead listing all elected officers' names, titles, and email addresses. (For DocuSign purposes) The letter also had to identify who the signer (s) on the account would be, and it had to be signed and dated.

For those reasons, try calling before applying for the business bank account so you know what paperwork is needed to avoid delays in opening the account. This will be super helpful when establishing payment methods for your website and payment providers for your donors and fundraising events.

9. Apply for your 501(c)(3) tax-exempt status using IRS Form 1023.

If you're going the public charity route and looking for the filing status most donors give to, this is the way to go. Because my foundation was new, small, and didn't bring in much money, I was eligible to file the 1023EZ Form.

The IRS has a 1023 EZ Eligibility Worksheet you can use to verify if your foundation qualifies to file the regular form or the EZ form. **If you answer Yes to any *of the worksheet questions, specifically if you anticipate your annual gross receipts will exceed $50,000 in the next 3 years, you will have to complete the regular 1023 form, which can be lengthy and more expensive.***

Once you receive your approval, it's permanent as long as you manage and submit your required documents (990 Form) and file the applicable state forms. You'll only have to do it once, as long as it's done right. It is not required to resubmit the 1023 form after raising more money.

Note: There are a ton of 501©s out there that are NOT 501©3s. AARP (American Association of Retired Persons) and the NAACP (National Association for the Advancement of Colored People), for example, are both 501©4 organizations that receive most of their funding through membership dues. Consult with a tax attorney and any other legal professional to determine which tax-exempt status works best for your foundation.

I've received a lot of questions about Grant Filing rules with a pending 501c3 application, so I'll break this down:

1. *Can you apply for a grant while applying for tax-exempt status?* Technically, yes, but there's a caveat. It's advised that you disclose the foundations' uncertain tax status either on the grant application or with a letter using the disclaimer something to the effect of ***The Craig D. Butler Scholarship Foundation is a Pennsylvania nonprofit organization in the process of applying for 501c3 status.*** Most donors who are laid back won't mind taking the risk that their donation may not be deductible, but most established donors and grant holders may not.

2. *What is the filing timeframe?* In order for your organization to receive tax-deductible donations retroactively while your 501c3 registration is pending, the IRS states that an organization must apply within 27 months from the end of the month in which the organization was formed. If this is done, the organization may be acknowledged as exempt from the date of formation. If an organization files for tax-exempt status after the 27-month

deadline, the exempt status may only be accepted from the filing date forward.

*Cautionary Tip:

Yes, you can receive tax-deductible donations retroactively while your 501c3 registration is pending; however, if you're denied is when things can go left:

1. Donors aren't eligible to claim the deduction if you have to refile more than once, and it extends past the tax year.

2. Certain organizations, especially grants from private or local organizations, won't have that assurance and could choose another applicant over you, or you may be considered ineligible for the grant.

3. There's also the possibility that an organization completes an application expecting to be a public charity but may be classified as a private foundation.

4. The more considerable concern is compliance with the state. Recall page 17 for the charity registration section, where you'll have to complete a state form to solicit donations. In PA, they asked if you have the 501c3 and if you've ever been denied.

a) Unless you've applied or know someone who has, I would HIGHLY recommend using an attorney or filing service to complete this form on your behalf. It can be complicated, costly, and time-consuming, and I was denied the first time I applied because I had one question wrong. This isn't like most documents where you'll receive a courtesy call informing you of your errors: They will deny you, send you a denial letter, refund your fee, and send you on your merry way until you get the courage to apply again. The process can take anywhere from two months to one year if you do this yourself, and during the pandemic shutdown, it took twice the time. The second time I applied, I used SwyftFilings to complete my 1023EZ and paid to expedite the service. I received approval two months later, and I haven't looked back.

b) Remember to save, file, and keep your 501c3 determination letter close. You will be asked for a copy of this document A LOT! I've submitted a copy of this form when applying for grants, state registration documents, and even to vendors to provide discounts.

10. Create your scholarship's branding (logo, brand colors, social media).

When brainstorming how you want your brand to look, you want to think of the identity you want to convey to the public and your purpose. Maybe you have a specific color, logo, or slogan in mind, but you'll want to concentrate on how you want the world to see you. This is, in essence, your foundation's calling card.

Think about why brands like Nike and Apple can provide individuals with a product that's not only valuable but also visible. These brands are easily recognizable, and that's the goal you should aim for. You may have already begun this step if you started creating your website. Now, I was fortunate enough to have a friend who was a dope artist who designed my original logo, but I did hire a freelancer to design my professional branding. If you decide to hire a designer for anything, remember to obtain a copyright transfer agreement from the designer to ensure your brand can only be used by you.

I would also recommend creating your branding presence at least 12 weeks before your scholarship launches. This gives you time to create a buzz about your purpose and allows you to turn followers into donors.

Weeks 1 through 4 consist of

- ✓ Creating your social media pages for your foundation
- ✓ Hiring freelancers for your brand design, if necessary
- ✓ Starting an email list

For your social media accounts, begin posting upcoming events and milestone dates and find relevant pages to follow. I've found Facebook and Instagram to be the most helpful, mainly because of the number of groups they have available and the use of their donation button. LinkedIn is great for building your foundation's presence, and Twitter is great for connecting with the community. Begin to post content about your cause, additional resources, fun facts, etc. This is also the stage where you may be thinking about branding colors and slogans if you haven't yet developed your website.

Weeks 4 through 8

- ✓ Fine-tuning your website layout
- ✓ Deciding on content for your first newsletter
- ✓ Fine-tuning your brand's personality and tone.

During this phase, I did an informal beta-test amongst family, friends, and colleagues to give me their general first impression of the foundation so it could put me in their shoes. I wanted to ensure there wasn't a disconnect between our mission and our brands' personalities. Some of the feedback we received questioned if we were a gun violence nonprofit similar to CeaseFire or Everytown. I realized I needed to be concise about how I would earn my audiences' attention, that although the nature of the foundation is an after-effect to gun violence, the actual mission is educating our youth.

Weeks 8 through 12

- ✓ Positioning your foundation to the community, be it letters to the editor of a local newspaper, creating a press release, or reaching out to local elected officials. I wrote a press release to introduce our foundation and to highlight the need our nonprofit would solve. I also created a One-Pager to mail to schools and the city council as a direct mail initiative to reach my targeted audience.

Chapter 5

Budgeting – Funding – Bookkeeping....Oh My!

Budget

My sister and Irish twin is notorious for bussing on me and my 'obsession' with budgets. I'm talking years, y'all. If you called her right now and asked her what Khadijah was doing, 9 times out of 10, she would say "I don't know, somewhere looking at her budget." Well, sis, thanks to your teasing, I can pay it forward with my budget knowledge! No matter the structure of your scholarship or if you have an endearing family member or friend like my sister, there are quite a few costs involved with starting a scholarship foundation. One of the primary things you'll want to do is establish an annual budget for your scholarship. Depending on how big or small your budget is it will determine when you're ready to start your scholarship year.

If you have a small budget, you may only be able to afford the initial startup costs of setting up the business entity, computer and communication fees, legal fees, website, accounting, and consultant fees, etc., in your first year, which can range anywhere from $500 – 1,200. If funding isn't an issue, and you're ready to start your scholarship year, you'll want to add costs for advertising, marketing, postage, a P.O. box (If you don't have a physical location), and the amount you want to give the recipients. The costs can vary depending on how much your award will be.

For most small startup nonprofits, your first year of operations may be in your home, and in my case, I had no choice but to establish a home office when I started due to the COVID shutdown. If you want to begin thinking long-term about office space, you'll want to build a line item in your two to three-year budget to begin the planning phase. You can start slow by looking into virtual offices such as Regus or shared spaces from organizations like the Nonprofit Centers Network. Regus is an excellent alternative to a P.O. box if you want a physical business address and you want your mail sent there. Nonprofit Centers Network is a great resource for shared spaces, but you do have to be a member. Once you begin receiving steady donations, grants, and any other sources of revenue, you may want to start looking into purchasing a building by the five-year mark. For any additional resources, contact your state for referrals.

Funding

When funding your scholarship foundation, the questions to ask are:

1. Where will my primary source of revenue come from?
2. Will I, as the founder, have to use my savings until I receive funding?
3. Will I be receiving donations?
4. Will I have other revenue streams to use to fund the foundation?

Until you begin hosting fundraising events (which is an expense itself) or you start receiving grants, the answer to these questions will shape which funding method you choose.

Now, I will tell you that applying for grants is not only time-consuming but EXTREMELY competitive. It also takes at least your first year before you're even eligible since most organizations will ask for a copy of your 990 form and may even ask for a detailed budget. If you are going the grant route, this is vital when applying for your DUNS number.

For those who haven't heard of this term, the Data Universal Number System (DUNS) number is the first step in registering your foundation for grants. If you're going the private foundation route and you're not applying for grants, the DUNs numbers are typically not required. However, you should apply for one if you obtain the DUNS number to establish business credit or apply for a business loan.

As with the EIN, obtaining your DUNS number is free on the Dun & Bradstreet (D&B) website, or you can call the toll-free number. Let the agent know you are a federal grant/prospective applicant, and they will ask you to provide your legal name, headquarters name, address for your organization, telephone number, contact name and title, and the number of employees at your physical location. After you have provided all the details, they will immediately assign you a DUN'S number free of charge. I repeat, **DO NOT PAY FOR THIS SERVICE!**

Regarding the grant process, our foundation has received our DUNS and is registered on SAM and Grant.gov, but we haven't applied for government funding yet. We have applied for grants through platforms CyberGrants Frontdoor (Walmart), directly through the company's website (Costco), and a few local grant opportunities (CBS Philly). I keep track of all grant applications via a file on my computer organized by submission year. I plan to include a grant writer in next year's budget.

Charity Registration

Let's say you're lucky enough to receive a grant; yay! Not so fast on the celebration, chief! Some states will require you to register your charity to solicit donations. In the state of Pennsylvania, I had to complete a BCO-10 form. The Bureau of Corporations and Charitable Organizations 10 Form (BCO-10) is a state form that requires organizations soliciting donations from Pennsylvania residents to register with the state. The BCO-10 form is only needed if you didn't fill out a complete 990 form. Since you must accompany this registration form with your filed IRS-990N, I didn't register CDB Scholarship until I was one year in. I know, I know, you're probably saying, 'Khadijah, if I gotta file one more form?!' but think of it this way - it gives your donors a sense of security that your charity is not trying to trick its residents and credibility is everything!

Some donors may ask for a copy of your BCO-10 or go as far as researching it with your Secretary of State. A good rule of thumb is to develop a disclosure statement to supplement the BCO-10, informing your donors that the state can obtain information about your foundation if needed. Think of it as an informal announcement, a disclaimer that says, 'Don't worry, we legit!' Some state requirements allow you to record this on your website. It can look something to the effect of:

"The official registration and financial information of The Craig D. Butler Scholarship Foundation may be obtained from the Pennsylvania Department of State by calling toll-free, within Pennsylvania, 1 (800) 732-0999. Registration does not imply endorsement."

Note: If you have a national or regional foundation and are planning on soliciting multiple states, you must have a disclosure statement for EACH state.

Once again, check with your state on these requirements.

Bookkeeping

Maybe you're an Excel guru, or perhaps you're incredibly organized. Either way, you WILL need a bookkeeping system for your scholarship foundation. Trying to keep track of your foundation's financial actions without a system in place can be a nightmare if this is overlooked. This is typically the time when electing a financial officer or treasurer on your board will be of value. You may do this the moment you write your first check or your fifth, but it's good practice to begin looking into bookkeeping systems once your foundation's bank account is set up.

Most of your foundations' financial actions include tracking donations (cash or in-kind), managing invoices, and organizing receipts. Now, you can use bookkeeping software such as Zoho, Aplos, QuickBooks, or Excel Sheets. I'm a project manager by day, so manipulating an Excel sheet using pivot tables and all that jazz is my thing, but it doesn't have to be yours. As always, consult with an accountant on recommendations.

Chapter 6

Paperwork, Paperwork, Paperwork!

Eligibility Requirements

You've chosen your cause. Check. You've defined your mission, check. You've filled out every possible document known to man without pulling your hair out. Check! (I'm on my Jay Z "All I Need" vibe) Just one more piece of paperwork, it's the ultimate piece of paperwork.... Your Scholarship Application! Once you've verified the legal requirements of your cause, you'll want to begin defining the terms of your scholarship. These prerequisites should be available and accessible for your students to find. When determining the scholarships' eligibility, consider asking yourself the following questions:

1. How many scholarships will my foundation award?
2. Is this a one-time award or renewable?
3. How will students apply?

4. How much will each award be?

5. Will I disburse the award to the student or the university?

6. Should my foundation grant smaller awards to several recipients or fewer rewards of substance with a more significant impact?

7. When is the deadline?

8. When should my foundation open for applications?

Now, because my scholarship foundation appeals to a narrow demographic and a more defined community for Philadelphia residents, I open my application period in the fall. This allows me more time to evaluate applications, and there are fewer scholarship programs to compete with before financial aid season is in full swing in the spring.

Application Packet

Next, create your scholarship application packet and decide if you will offer a paper application or if your students will download the application on your website. I use both options to widen my reach.

There are pros and cons of online application packets vs. paper application packets:

▸ Students spend most of their day online with their heads buried in their phones, so downloading your application packet may be more convenient.

▸ When receiving an online application, it's simpler for me to file it in a folder on my computer vs. the paper copy being physically filed. Now, I do like my paper applications, selor or other school organization on our behalf.

▸ Students eliminate the need to pay to mail the application and potentially avoid missing the timeline if it is post-marked late. This was an issue a few years ago due to Covid, and now the shipping times, in general, are longer.

There are a ton of templates you can google, or if you're creative, you can make your own. One jew-el, the longer the application, the less chance you have for a student to apply. Design the application with enough detail that's succinct but doesn't discourage them from quitting midway.

When designing your application packet, think about what you want to include. Besides your basic demographics and high school details, consider AP courses, community activities, athletics, and part-time jobs - whatever your foundation values in an applicant. For the metrics of our applicants, I took more of an unorthodox approach to selecting our winners.

First, I evaluated the ratio of applicants received vs eligible applicants. Since we award two scholarships yearly, I aimed to receive at least five applications, but we wound up receiving nine. Two of the applicants were not eligible since they were out of state, and two of the applicants had incomplete application packets.

Second, I looked at more than just the weighted GPA; I looked at the types of classes they were enrolled in. All of the applicants were taking AP courses and receiving A's in all of them.

Thirdly, I looked at their activities and jobs to see if they were prepared to balance the world of college life. All applicants worked part-time, participated in sports, and actively participated in extracurricular activities.

Fourth, I looked at family data to see what additional hurdles the student struggled with and if they've been exposed to some form of gun violence and still preserved. All applicants either had multiple siblings, lived in a high-crime area, came from single-parent households, or had parents who migrated from other countries.

Fifth, we did not provide an essay word count; we wanted to give students the latitude to write as much or as little as possible as long as the essay included Substance, Organization, Style, and Correctness. For instance, Does the essay create interest? Is there quality/quantity of evidence? Is there a unified flow of paragraphs and sentences? Are there grammar, spelling, and punctuation errors? We wanted to see how much the students have learned and if they can apply their knowledge in college.

Lastly, the reference letters and phone calls to the guidance counselors gave me an overall picture of the student who best represented the Craig D. Butler Scholarship award. Hearing the school staff advocate for their students in a way that didn't translate into their application packet is synonymous with a job interview. It gives your board a better idea of the student's character and clarifies details that may be missing in the application.

SATs/ACTs – Now, I'm not going to date myself, but SAT/ACT prep was massive when I was in high school, and a lot of weight was put on your complete acceptance packet. However, I recently learned that after starting this foundation, most universities are now reviewing applicants on a more holistic level. SAT/ACT scores are now test-optional, especially when most testing centers shut down during Covid. I reached out to a few local universities and guidance counselors who had strong opinions on most students not being taught most of the concepts provided in these tests, and some of these students, especially those from the underserved populations I serve, may not be academically prepared to succeed at most of the colleges they are accepted to.

Jewel

Consider waiving SAT/ACT scores and include an checklist in the application packet.

Some colleges and universities still require test scores for admission, so I included in the application packet a disclaimer that test scores are required unless the university or college the student attends has a test-optional policy.

Application Packet Checklist - More than likely, the students applying for your scholarship will apply for many other scholarships. One of our recipients applied to over 85 scholarships alone! A simple checklist outlining what will be included in the application packet will keep your students more organized when submitting. Once again, a checklist can be pretty simple and informal to create. This can include the application, transcripts, letters of recommendation, essay, and anything else you want to include in your packet.

Chapter 7
Promoting Your Scholarship and Being Found

"Ready or Not, Here I Come, You Can't Hide, Gonna Find you, and Take it slowly!" ("Fugees – Ready or Not Lyrics |Genius Lyrics") The most crucial step in establishing a scholarship foundation is being found, Fugees style! You gotta have that same energy when promoting your scholarship. Being found, especially when you're new, not a celebrity, or don't have a big following, will take some time.

If you plan to award your scholarship locally, contact your city council members and local high schools, specifically guidance counselors and principals. I recommend positioning yourself to them at the beginning of the school year once your website and social media pages are available. Most high schools will have a dedicated page on their website, particularly for College Advising with the school counselors' contact details. Most have been happy to hear from our organization and will pass along your scholarship details to staff and students. They were a big help to our organization by listing us on the School District's website.

Registering your scholarship foundation on scholarship boards is MANDATORY! For example, Unigo, MyScholly, and Scholarships.com are excellent places to start.

Social media can be a huge help, especially since high school and college students spend a lot of time on major sites like Twitter, Facebook, and Instagram.

Your website is where your scholarship will live, and if you have a physical location, it will be easier for students to find you when connecting your geographic allocation.

One final option is to contact colleges and universities in the area for potential incoming first-year students who may have applied.

Chapter 8
Fundraising

I touched on fundraising in earlier chapters, but having a fundraising plan is critical when determining what strategies will be used to fund your scholarship award. Even if you are going the private foundation route and have a huge budget, you don't want to have a board meeting and have your officers throw out a slew of ideas without having an actual plan to execute them.

Your fundraising plan should include your overall goal, how much you want to raise, the strategy used to reach the goal, and how the fundraising event will be executed.

Let's say you want to raise $5,000 in your second year. Maybe $2,000 will come from grants, $1,000 from donors, $1,000 from a fundraising event, and $1,000 from online fundraising (i.e., Facebook Button and your foundation's website). A written fundraising plan keeps you and your board organized and gets you from A to Z.

There are a ton of ideas out there, but having more than one fundraising strategy each year is necessary. When COVID hit in 2020, we had to get creative since most venues closed due to a lack of revenue or only allowed a certain number of people in their venue. By this point, we had made it to our first full year in operation, and my fundraising goal was to have at least one event per year. We decided on a virtual auction, where we received in-kind donations from primarily local businesses and auctioned them using 32auctions.com. This virtual auction website made the silent auction user-friendly and painless. Now, you can use your website to manage and host your silent auction if you choose, but what I discovered about using this site is it opened me up to receive discounts on my payment methods as a nonprofit.

Stripe and PayPal were the payment vendors that 32auctions used to complete transactions. Because I ask a lot of questions in general, I reached out to Stripe and informed them I was a nonprofit and asked if a discount was offered. Stripe informed me my foundation was eligible for a discount on the transaction fee, 2.2% vs. 2.9% for a for-profit business. PayPal already provided us with a charity transaction rate of 1.99% vs. 3.49% for a for-profit company. The moral of the story is that if I didn't have an event and didn't ask questions, I wouldn't have known what I was eligible for until I asked.

Since my foundation serves Philadelphia residents, we have at least one in-person event to connect with the community and establish credibility, and you should, too! For someone who is a naturally private, subdued individual, I discovered early on that people want to know who you are and connect with you as an individual, put a face to the brand, and establish trust before they part ways with their money. No matter the fundraising method, a walkathon, a t-shirt campaign, or a recurring gift, it starts with a fundraising plan.

Chapter 9

Selecting Your Winners

Once the application deadline closes, your board will become the real-life Shark Tank, America's Next Top Model, and The Voice, all in one! It is the stage when the real work begins and when your board turns into official Scholarship Judges. Selecting your winners takes time, deliberation, evaluation, confirmation, and notification. I know I just went all Dr. Seuss on y'all, but allow me to elaborate! 😊 😊

Time – It took about four weeks overall with the selection process. This included assembling the board, narrowing down the finalists, speaking to references, and retrieving supplemental documentation.

Deliberation - Having a diverse board is what makes the deliberation process impactful. You want board members who can be objective and will provide unique perspectives on the students you're supporting.

Evaluation – When evaluating applications, deciding what scale you are using, if any, will guide your board in choosing the best recipient. My foundation did not use a formal grading scale per se since our mission is rooted in extraordinary circumstances; however, typical program factors you can start with include GPA, School/Volunteer activities, Letters of Recommendation, essays, etc.

Confirmation – Depending on the eligibility requirements of your scholarship foundation, confirming that the applicants meet those requirements is crucial. Maybe it's confirming they're still attending high school or simply requesting a copy of their acceptance letter from the university. You want to ensure the applicant you're considering is still eligible if you need to choose an alternate.

Notification - The selection process should consider notifying the winners through a phone call, zoom meeting, face-to-face, or certified mail. News like this should be celebrated in a medium that's a bit more personal than an email. This will also allow you to put the face and voice to the application.

Let me tell you, our selection process was a challenge for our board, and it was such a significant problem to have! It was a proud moment. It solidified my decision to start my foundation and verified the genuine need of students in the community who wanted to receive an education if cost wasn't a factor.

According to Data USA, African American students in Philadelphia only make up 14% of degrees awarded compared to 57% of White students In Philadelphia. I already planned to start a foundation that served Philadelphia since it is my hometown, and my father graduated from a Philadelphia school, but seeing such a vast education gap for minority youth was sad and disappointing. When I saw our first-year applicants were honors students, had high GPAs, and worked part-time, amongst other stand-out qualities, I felt like a proud mama! The moral of the story: This is the moment when the effort of filling out paperwork, fundraising, and all other arduous tasks leading you up to this point will make your decision to start a scholarship foundation worthwhile.

A couple of jew-els to pass along:

1. Once your scholarship recipients are selected, it's good practice to notify those applicants who were not chosen. It took a lot of time and effort for these students to apply to your program, and they deserve to know the outcome, even if they weren't chosen. I sent each applicant a letter thanking them and wishing them luck in their future degree pursuit.

2. When evaluating your applicants, really consider which student is an accurate representation of your foundation. Try not to get too caught up on quantitative factors like who's GPA was higher or how many activities the student was involved in. Think about the whole package and what

it will mean to give those students a shot who may not have had one. One of our applicants stood out because she was an entrepreneur attending an HBCU and had the greatest need as an out-of-state student. Her guidance counselor praised her accomplishments, which was the determining factor. Scholarships create a path of opportunity, propelling the student to soar.

Chapter 10
Awarding the Scholarship

Awarding the scholarship was the most rewarding experience for me as a founder. To hear the joy and excitement in the students' voices took me back to the lyrics "I reminisce, I reminisce" by Pete Rock and CL Smooth the day I started the foundation. When I think of the song's origin, how it pays respect to loved ones, and how our family reminisces about my father, granting those first awards in his honor brings everything full circle.

There are a few housekeeping items you want to take care of when informing your recipients they have won the award:

1. Confirm with the student if the university they listed in the application packet is the one they decided to attend. One recipient listed one university on her application packet in December but received a scholarship from

another in March. If there is a change, retrieve a copy of the acceptance letter from the university the student has decided on.

2. By this point, you should have decided whether you would disburse the scholarship funds directly to the institution or the student. This must be outlined in your application packet, website, and any other correspondence from your foundation. With our scholarship, I chose to disburse the funds directly to the university, but I have seen other foundations issue a check directly to the student, and I learned why this may be the best option.

   a) Let's say you have a recipient who's received multiple scholarships and grants, and the financial aid office advises that including your scholarship award may make them ineligible for grants/awards received from the institution. Here is when you can consider allowing the scholarship to be applied in diverse ways. The student may use it to cover other educational expenses such as books, lab fees, or room/board. Maybe they can use it towards the following semester or split the award into both semesters. Whatever the case, discern which is the best fit for the recipient.

   b) If you decide to disburse the funds to the university directly, reach out to the institution BEFORE the semester ends so you can receive further instructions on distributing the funds in the student's best interest. Jot down the contact's name, mailing address, date of disbursement, and the semester the scholarship award will be applied for. This is critical if you cannot reach the financial aid office and must contact another staff member. We ran into a problem with this for one of our recipients, and it caused a delay in receiving her award. Most of the university staff were unavailable before the semester ended, and we had to wait until the beginning of the semester before we finally got in touch with someone.

c) However you disburse the funds, I recommend a certified check rather than writing a check from the foundation's account. Certified checks are more secure and less susceptible to fraud, and your bank usually personalizes them with the recipient's name and student ID. It's also beneficial during bookkeeping so you can maintain a separate record.

Chapter 11

Triumphs and Challenges

It's been five years since the Craig D. Butler Scholarship Foundation was established, and there are quite a few triumphs but just as many challenges I've experienced that I hope you can avoid:

1. COVID, Corona, or whoever you want to call her, threw a wrench in the initial startup of our scholarship foundation.

The triumph – having the fortitude to finally start the foundation, despite the emotional battles with reopening wounds of the loss of my father.

The challenge – two months after I started the nonprofit, we experienced a global shutdown in March 2020.

Since all the high schools were shut down, it eliminated the opportunity for us to connect with the principals and guidance counselors in person. We had postcards mailed out to the schools in February, which were later returned in April. The workaround was connecting with the schools via social media, email, and phone calls until the fall school year.

COVID also had a significant impact on in-person fundraising events. With the Delta and Omicron variants, most venues limited the number of guests allowed and required proof of vaccination, reducing the amount of donations your foundation could receive. As mentioned earlier, we did shift our fundraising plans to a virtual silent auction during the coronavirus shutdown, and it was a safe and convenient option; however, we lost out on establishing a deeper connection with our donors and keeping supporters engaged when we didn't have an in-person event.

The takeaway is there will always be something beyond your control that may discourage you, but learning to pivot despite your hurdles builds character.

2. Using an attorney or filing services like Swyft Filings/Legal Zoom to expedite the 501c3 process.

The triumph - Getting your 501c3 status, as mentioned in earlier chapters, is your gateway to so many benefits. The faster you have this, the better off you'll be. As mentioned, I applied and was denied after having one question wrong. But using Swyft Filings brought me back into the game.

The challenge – Delaying the filing cost me valuable time. Had I used Swyft Filings from the beginning, I could have received my tax-exempt status way earlier than planned. There's a higher probability you'll receive your approval when hiring these professionals since they complete a ton of these filings daily. I'm not deterring you from filing this yourself, but if there's one less thing you can remove off your plate, this would be the one task you should delegate.

3. Activating your Network

The concept of Activating my Network truly takes on so many meanings. The power of my network, be it friends, family, colleagues, or mentors, has genuinely shaped the trajectory of my scholarship program. I cannot count how often I have received constructive feedback, counsel, praise, and even downright frankness to make sure the foundation was operating at its best.

The triumph – My network has provided valuable insight and advice, even in the most unusual places. They have served as my source of humility, fortitude, and encouragement to push my cause through to see results.

The challenge – Accepting that some people in your network will not support the vision.

There's an unconscious expectation that your family and friends who love and care for you will be your biggest supporters when you pursue a goal. But the harsh reality is that just because you have a lot of likes and followers doesn't mean you will get the kind of support you expect. Most people won't have the courage to start a business, let alone a nonprofit organization. Most non-business owners will never have your vision or perspective, so being in your feelings about their level of support is futile. Why would you even want to convince someone of your purpose when you wouldn't be confident of theirs? There isn't a person on this planet who could convince me to sit back idle watching thousands of young adults forgo their opportunity to attend college is ok.

I've also learned that a lack of support from some may be egotistical – your success magnifies the lack of success in themselves. Sometimes, the way you move reminds others of their failures.

Finally, I learned that a person's lack of support might reflect how your absence affects them. Running your own business comes with a level of sacrifice most non-entrepreneurs will never understand. It will mean the time you may have spent hanging out will be spent working on your business. It will mean the money and effort you may have spent supporting them in the past will cease, and some will not join you in your journey nor acknowledge that being selfish is an indirect lack of support.

The point is make moves, push forward, and do whatever you have to. While disheartening at first, you will persevere.

4. Gaining Credibility – Now, we, as entrepreneurs, know the importance of credibility, especially if you're a new business AND an online business. Think about how the core of your scholarship program is to secure funding, be it corporations, donors, investors, or through grants. How would you convince a company to invest in your foundation without proof of concept?

The triumph – Listing my scholarship foundation on as many scholarship sites as possible.

The challenge – The process and effort to be listed to gain credibility can be cumbersome. Guidestar and Facebook (Now called Meta) are highly credible sources, but I struggled with being listed on both sites.

If you're using Facebook as a business account, they offer qualifying nonprofits a donate button to fundraise directly from Facebook and Instagram. It's an excellent tool, especially if it's the social platform of your primary audience. The issue lies during the verification process. It took almost two months to receive this badge due to confirmation needed from my bank, including their logo and official contact info, my charitable purpose, and even details about me as the principal officer of my foundation. They asked about my charity's goals, how I plan to achieve them, my mission statement, and even what causes my charity supports. I received a denial email literally every week for two months, and I was beyond the point of frustration and ready to give up. In some respects, I understand entirely the need to prevent fraud and scammers from collecting money, but I also wasn't prepared for that struggle. Ultimately, it made me more resilient, but most importantly, it taught me to accept how much follow-up action would always be needed.

Guidestar is a nonprofit's digital guidebook of sorts. It's where most donors can look up your nonprofit based on your profile and filings from your 990. Its mission is to provide as much transparency to the public as possible. FYI, before you can begin applying for credible sources such as the Facebook Donation Button, they will use GuideStar's info to validate your nonprofit, so you may want to wait until your Guidestar profile is complete before applying for these kinds of resources. The process was prolonged because of the COVID shutdown, but it was also due to the language being used. They wanted to confirm my EIN and Articles of Incorporation, but they used the term Letter of Affirmation in their email correspondence. At the time, I was only used to hearing the document described as an IRS determination letter. Once again, I didn't have a guide to tell me terminology or how a form should be completed, and the lack of knowledge and staff at these places during the shutdown made this an arduous task. The moral of the story is that patience is the ultimate virtue when establishing credibility.

5. Matching Gift Programs – There are a ton of corporations that commit to what's called corporate social responsibility that will 'match a gift' as an employee benefit. When an employee donates to a nonprofit organization, some employers will provide matching gifts on the employee's behalf to double their contribution.

The triumph – A few of our family and friends contacted their employers to match their donations to our foundation.

The challenge – Only certain companies participate or may only donate to specific charities. Here's when having a dope network has its advantages. Your family and friends may see an email about matching donations and submit a request to their employer to find out if your foundation is eligible. Have your donors check their employers' guidelines on when the funds will be sent to your nonprofit. Sometimes, employers use certain times during the year when the match will be processed. We received two matching gifts, both made in January and February, but we didn't receive the funds from the employer until May and June, respectively.

Jewel

Spark Good and iGive incentives your donors

One other jew-el – Using donation programs such as SparkGood and iGive to incentivize your donors.

I found out about SparkGood by accident. I applied for a Walmart Grant when I received a reply that while I didn't receive the grant, there were tools and resources I was eligible for as a nonprofit. Walmart's Spark Good Round-Up program allows customers who shop on Walmart.com or the Walmart App to round up their change to donate to the cause of their choice. Every little bit helps and most definitely adds up!

It doesn't cost anything for your donors to sign up, and it's an excellent way for them to give back effortlessly if they frequent Walmart.

iGive is a platform similar to SparkGood that donates a percentage of your purchases, except it's done with your favorite retailers. If you've ever used Rakuten, it's the same concept; it's basically a Rakuten for charities! Every time you shop at over 2300 retailers, iGive provides a percentage of what you spend to your favorite charity. You're donating while you're shopping without feeling guilty about it! And it's not just for apparel; it's for travel, restaurants, and even purchases you can make as a board member! I've used it to purchase business cards, printer ink, and office supplies. This is an easy service with which to get your donors on board!

6. Nonprofit Resources Galore!

This section is only going to apply to public charities. Once my 501c3 was approved, the floodgates opened for the number of available resources. I'm already a woman who cuts coupons, so getting discounts on my foundation was like receiving my new discount grocery shopping card!

The triumph – Using organizations such as SCORE, Catchafire, TechSoup, and Hello Alice to advance the foundation.

The challenge – Knowing they exist.

I did a TON of research, followed several social media channels, and even networked with a few people to find these, but it wasn't easy or instantaneous. My rule of thumb was that once I found a resource, I stopped what I was doing and immediately visited the website, social media page, and whatever medium was offered so I wouldn't miss the opportunity.

TechSoup is a non-profit organization that offers donated and discounted technology products. I received a half-price discount on my website hosting for two years! But it's only for 501c3 exempt organizations.

SCORE is a non-profit organization that assists small businesses and newly formed organizations with many resources. They have a host of volunteers local to your area and will assign a mentor to guide you through questions you may have. My mentor was instrumental in assisting me with filing my first 990 form. SCORE provides a ton of webinars, free resources, local events, and workshops covering topics ranging from marketing to social media, as well as website design.

<u>Hello Alice</u> helps other small businesses grow via community groups, access to funding, including grants for nonprofit and for-profit companies, and essential day-to-day tools for your business.

<u>Catchafire</u>, another nonprofit organization, has been phenomenal for my foundation! Catchafire pairs volunteers to work on projects for your foundation to help you grow. I've had a ton of tasks completed, and they were all free! A press release, Organizational One Pager, Donor Letters, Partnership Proposal Presentation, and Website Updates! This resource is also for 501c3 organizations only.

NOTE: Going the private foundation route doesn't mean there aren't just as many resources as the private charity option. I have seen a few grants I wasn't eligible for because I am a nonprofit, so I didn't spend much time looking into it, but they do exist.

There are many resources out there; you just need to know where to look and ask questions.

7. Be Patient!

I've been told I'm an overachiever, can't sit still, and that sitting on my hands is a foreign concept. It can be a gift and a curse, honestly.

The triumph – Being patient allowed me to focus on other details to propel my foundation.

The challenge – Problems arise when you don't take your time. As you can see, I've made many mistakes; some were due to a lack of knowledge, but others were due to a lack of patience. Anything worth having takes time, and sometimes, we must trust that. You don't want to rush the development of your foundation because you have this artificial timeline in your head. You'll end up overlooking something or missing an opportunity altogether. Take your time with everything! You may want to focus on establishing your brand and visibility in your first year. Maybe you want to focus on fine-tuning your scholarship application packet. Whatever the case, understand your first and second year may be the pilot, but there's the opportunity for you and your board to assess what worked and what didn't.

Being patient also means just living in the moment of your dopeness. Do you know how rare and unique you are that you have made a conscious decision to give the gift of education to others? Bringing awareness to a cause important to you and your community is nothing short of amazing! When I think of my vision for the Craig D. Butler Scholarship Foundation, I'm on my Rick Ross. "I'm building a dream with elevators in it!" I strive to make merit scholarships in Philadelphia a believable reality. Despite the education achievement gap for minority and low-income students, our recipients can change the narrative from high school graduates to college attendees.

Jewel

Live and revel in your accomplishment!

To my future scholarship foundation founders, my last jew-el for you: Live and revel in how great of an accomplishment it is, and when the time is right, everything will fall into place.

About the Author

Khadijah Butler

Born and raised in Philadelphia, PA, Khadijah Butler is an Around-the-Way girl with a thirst for knowledge and a hunger for education equality amongst minorities. She is the founder and president of the Craig D. Butler Scholarship Foundation, with a B.S. in Kinesiology from Temple University and an M.S. in Management from Rosemont College.

Strong, Brave, Fierce, Full of Fire & Vigor, she looks every challenge dead in the eye and gives them a wink. When she is not writing or managing the foundation, she is amplifying her voice to remove economic hurdles for college-bound students in Philadelphia.

About the
Craig D. Butler
Scholarship Foundation

The Craig D. Butler Scholarship Foundation was established in January 2020 to honor the life of Craig D. Butler, for whom the scholarship is named, and to continue his legacy of integrity, generosity, and service. Craig was a dedicated husband and father of three, a true pillar of the Philadelphia community. He also served his country as a Pneumatic Tool Operator in the United States Navy. His charismatic energy, love for his family, ability to break out in song for no apparent reason, and tenacity to stand firm in his principles were the essence of who he was. Considering what would have been Craig's 64th birthday, the Butler family organized this annual scholarship in his memory.

CDB Scholarships' mission is to provide financial assistance to African American high school seniors in Pennsylvania pursuing higher education in the aftermath of gun violence. Our cardinal principle is to ensure minorities from underserved populations are not economically disadvantaged to receive a quality education. In addition to the scholarship, the CDB Foundation rallies for gun reform and education advocacy.

Since 2024, our foundation has awarded ten scholarships to deserving youth with outstanding achievements. Our commitment to our community to bridge education inequality and mobilize economic growth amongst minorities is boundless.

To learn more, visit us at www.craigdbutlerscholarship.com

(267)362-9082

1500 Chestnut Street, Suite 2, ATTN # 1194

Philadelphia, PA 19102

Follow the Craig D. Butler Scholarship Foundation on Social Media

  @cdbscholarship

Kind Regards,

The Craig D. Butler Scholarship Foundation

Contact Us!

Are you or anyone you know interested in sponsoring or partnering with Craig D. Butler Scholarship, or you have a high school student eligible for a scholarship? If so, we look forward to hearing from you!

Resources & Checklists

IRS 1023 EZ – Internal Revenue Service (2021, November) *About Form 1023 EZ. https://www.irs.gov/forms-pubs/about-form-1023-ez*

IRS Publication 3833 – Disaster Relief, Providing Assistance through Charitable Organizations. (2019, December) *https://www.irs.gov/pub/irs-pdf/p3833.pdf*

Employer Identification Number (EIN) – Internal Revenue Service (2021, November) *Apply for an Employer Identification Number (EIN) Online. https://www.irs.gov/businesses/small-businesses-selfemployed/apply-for-an-employer-identification-numberein-online*

Dun & Bradstreet (D&B) (2021, November) *Dun & Bradstreet D-U-N-S number* https://www.dnb.com/duns-number.html

Harbor Compliance – *Nonprofit Governance by State* (2020, September 9) https://www.harborcompliance.com/information/nonproft-governance-by-state

Nonprofit Centers Network – Offers shared spaces for nonprofits

Regus – (2021, November) *Virtual Offices. https://www.regus.com/en-us/virtual-offices*

SCORE - https://www.score.org/

Catchafire - https://www.catcha re.org/

TechSoup - https://www.techsoup.org/

QuickBooks – (2021, November) *Nonprofit accounting software solution* - https://quickbooks.intuit.com/industry/non-pro its/

Zohos (2021, November) *One-stop solution for all your nonprofit management needs.* https://www.zoho.com/creator/nonpro itsmanagement-software/

Aplos (2021, November) *Manage your finances, people & giving for your nonprofit or church. https://www.aplos.com/*

Hello Alice https://helloalice.com/

iGive - https://www.igive.com/welcome/lp16/cr64a.cfm

System Award Management (SAM) https://sam.gov/content/home

BoardSource - https://boardsource.org/

Boardable - https://boardable.com/

Grants.gov https://www.grants.gov/

Guidestar - https://www.guidestar.org/

UNIGO - https://www.unigo.com/scholarships/ourscholarships

MyScholly - https://myscholly.com/

Scholarships.com - https://www.scholarships.com/

Petersons - https://www.petersons.com/scholarshipsearch.aspx

Upwork - https://www.upwork.com/

Fiverr - https://www. iverr.com/

32auctions - https://www.32auctions.com/

PayPal for Nonprofits - https://www.paypal.com/us/webapps/mpp/nfp

Stripe – (2021, November) *Fee discount for nonprofit organizations.*
https://support.stripe.com/questions/fee-discount-fornonprofit-organizations

Data USA – *2019 Student and Race Ethnicity Groups Degrees Awarded.* https://datausa.io/profile/geo/philadelphia-pa

Charity Registration – (2021, November) *Pennsylvania*

Department of State Bureau of Corporations and Charitable Organizations (BCO-10 Form) - https://www.dos.pa.gov/ BusinessCharities/Charities/Resources/Documents/BCO- 10% 20 inal%20instructions%201-2018.pdf

Council of Foundations – www.cof.org

Laying the Foundation
Brick by Brick: The Playlist

Introduction
"Survival of the Fittest" by Mobb Deep and Sick of It All

Chapter 2 Private Foundation vs. Public Charity
"Aint No Half-Steppin" by Big Daddy Kane

Chapter 3 Choosing Your Board
"Slow Down" by Brand Nubian

Chapter 6 Paperwork, Paperwork, Paperwork!
"All I Need" by Jay Z

Chapter 7 Promoting Your Scholarship
"Ready or Not" by The Fugees

Chapter 10 Awarding the Scholarship
"They Reminisce Over You (T.R.O.Y.)" by Pete Rock & CL Smooth

Chapter 11 Triumphs and Challenges
"Push It" by Rick Ross

I do not own the rights to any song listed above. They were my inspirations during those late nights and early mornings of writing. To the artists, thank you for propelling me to get these words on the page.

Sample Board
Meeting Agenda

CDB SCHOLARSHIP
THE DREAM LIVES ON

Craig D. Butler Scholarship Board Meeting

Thursday, 02.27.2020
1:30 pm EST

Attendees
TBD, *President*
TBD, *Secretary*
TBD, *Treasurer*

Agenda

New Business
1. Determine Monthly Meeting Frequency
2. Fundraising Events - Applebees, Bowling
3. ByLaws Review
4. Foundation Endorsements
5. Advertising/Promotional Ideas

Notes

- ▸ Pending student records follow-up from WP High Records Management.
- ▸ First Company Launch event tentative for August 2020; Details TBD.
  - ○ Vendors to confirm if 501c3 is required to book an event.

Action Items

1. Mission Statement to be finalized.

Next Meeting Agenda Items

- ▸ Photos - Social media/Senior Class Photo to be included
  in the application packet.
- ▸ Complete - 2-year accounting expenses.
- ▸ Donation Cards to account during gala - Who monitors?

CDB SCHOLARSHIP
THE DREAM LIVES ON

Sample Scholarship Application

2024-25 CDB Scholarship Foundation

Application

APPLICATION PACKET CHECKLIST

_____ Scholarship Application

_____ Official Transcript

_____ Copy of your SAT or ACT scores

_____ Two (2) Recommendations (Forms Attached)

_____ Typewritten Essay

_____ Make sure your name is on all attachments.

Sample Bylaws

CORPORATE BYLAWS

OF

CDB Scholarship Foundation

These general bylaws have been customized to fit your company's information. These Bylaws should be reviewed and edited by the company's Board of Directors or attorney to meet your company's specific needs and to conform to any statutory changes before adoption.

Table of Contents

ARTICLE 1---ORGANIZATION 1
  1.1 PRINCIPAL OFFICE. 1
  1.2 REGISTERED AGENT. 1
  1.3 GOVERNING INSTRUMENTS. 1
ARTICLE 2--- PURPOSE, OBJECTIVES, AND MEMBERSHIP 2
  2.1 CHARITABLE, EDUCATIONAL, RELIGIOUS AND
  SCIENTIFIC PURPOSES. 2
  2.2 INUREMENT OF INCOME. 2
  2.3 LEGISLATIVE OR POLITICAL ACTIVITIES. 2
  2.4 OPERATIONAL LIMITATIONS. 2
  2.5 NONDISCRIMINATION POLICY. 2
  2.6 MEMBERSHIP. 3

ARTICLE 3---BOARD OF DIRECTOR MEETING   **3**

   3.1 MEETING LOCATION.   3

   3.2 REGULAR MEETINGS.   3

   3.3 SPECIAL MEETINGS.   3

   3.4 TELEPHONE MEETINGS.   3

   3.5 ACTION WITHOUT A MEETING.   3

   3.6 QUORUM.   4

ARTICLE 4---DIRECTORS   **4**

   4.1 AUTHORITY.   4

   4.2 ELECTION.   4

   4.3 NUMBER OF DIRECTORS.   4

   4.4 RESIGNATION.   4

   4.5 VACANCIES.   5

   4.6 COMPENSATION.   5

ARTICLE 5---OFFICERS   **5**

   5.1 NUMBER OF OFFICERS.   5

   5.2 ELECTION.   5

   5.3 REMOVAL AND RESIGNATION.   5

   5.4 PRESIDENT.   6

   5.5 SECRETARY.   6

   5.6 COMPENSATION.   6

ARTICLE 6---AUTHORITY TO EXECUTE   **6**

   6.1 BINDING POWER.   6

   6.2 SIGNATORIES.   6

ARTICLE 7---DISSOLUTION   **7**

ARTICLE 8---CORPORATE RECORDS   **7**

   8.1 CORPORATE MINUTES.   7

   8.2 FINANCIAL RECORDS.   7

   8.3 INSPECTION OF RECORDS.   7

   8.4 FISCAL YEAR.   7

ARTICLE 9---INDEMNIFICATION AND INSURANCE   **8**

   9.1 INDEMNIFICATION.   8

   9.2 INSURANCE.   8

ARTICLE 10---ADOPTION   **8**

CORPORATE BYLAWS

OF

CDB Scholarship Foundation

Article 1---Organization

1.1 PRINCIPAL OFFICE.

The Board of Directors will determine the principal office of the Corporation. Other offices may also be established at places the Board deems necessary for business conduct. A copy of these bylaws will be kept at the principal office.

1.2 REGISTERED AGENT.

The name and address of the Registered Agent are provided in the Articles of Incorporation that was filed with the Secretary of State. The Registered Agent may only be changed by filling out the appropriate paperwork with the Secretary of State. The Board must approve each change of Registered Agent of Directors.

1.3 GOVERNING INSTRUMENTS.

The Corporation will operate under the Articles of Incorporation and Bylaws requirements. The Board of Directors may amend the Bylaws.

Article 2--- Purpose, Objectives, and Membership

2.1 CHARITABLE, EDUCATIONAL, RELIGIOUS AND SCIENTIFIC PURPOSES.

The Corporation is organized exclusively for charitable, educational, religious, or scientific purposes within the meaning of Section 501(c)(3) of the Internal Revenue Code. The Corporation's specific purpose is:

2.2 INUREMENT OF INCOME.

The income of the Corporation shall not be distributed to or used for the benefit of its members, directors, officers, or other persons except that the Corporation is authorized to pay reasonable compensation for services rendered.

2.3 LEGISLATIVE OR POLITICAL ACTIVITIES.

The Corporation shall not participate in or intervene in any political campaign on behalf of any candidate for public office or dedicate a substantial part of its activities to propaganda or attempts to influence legislation.

2.4 OPERATIONAL LIMITATIONS.

The Corporation shall not conduct or participate in any activities not permitted to be carried on by a tax-exempt 501(c)(3) corporation or by a corporation whose contributions are deductible under Section 170(c)(2) of the IRS code of 1954 or the corresponding provision of any future US Internal Revenue Law.

2.5 NONDISCRIMINATION POLICY.

Unlawful discrimination based on sex, age, race, color, national origin, religion, physical handicap, or disability will not be permitted or tolerated by the Corporation.

2.6 MEMBERSHIP.
The Corporation will not have members.

Article 3---Board of Director Meeting

3.1 MEETING LOCATION.
Meetings shall be held at the Corporation's principal place of business or an alternate location chosen by the Board.

3.2 REGULAR MEETINGS.
Regular Meetings shall be held at a date and time that is acceptable to the Board members and at a frequency that promotes the growth of the Corporation.

3.3 SPECIAL MEETINGS.
Special meetings may be called at any time by the president of the Board of Directors. Each must receive notice from the meeting Director at least 3 days before the meeting. The notice must include the agenda for the meeting along with the place and time of the meeting.

3.4 TELEPHONE MEETINGS.
When necessary or desired, the Board may elect to meet via conference call or any other means where all participants can hear each other. Decisions made at such meetings will have the same authority and power as decisions made at meetings where the participants are physically present.

3.5 ACTION WITHOUT A MEETING.
Any action that may be taken at a regular or special meeting of the Board may be taken without a meeting if all members of the Board, in writing, consent to the action. All such actions will have

the same authority and power as actions passed at meetings where the participants were physically present.

3.6 QUORUM.

A majority of the authorized Directors will constitute a quorum. A quorum is required for actions taken to be considered Board approved.

Article 4---Directors

4.1 AUTHORITY.

The business and affairs of the Corporation shall be managed by a Board of Directors subject to any limitations in the Articles of Incorporation.

4.2 ELECTION.

The members of the Board of Directors will be elected by the voting members at the annual meeting. The Director will serve for the time specified at their election but no less than one year.

4.3 NUMBER OF DIRECTORS.

The Board will determine the number of authorized directors, but will not be less than three. This number may be increased or decreased as needed by a vote of the Board. No decrease in the number of Directors may shorten the term of an incumbent Director.

4.4 RESIGNATION.

At any time, a Director may resign by giving the Secretary of the Corporation a letter. The resignation will become effective immediately or at the date specified without a vote of the Board. A vote of a quorum of Directors will be required to remove a Director for cause.

4.5 VACANCIES.

A vote of the Board will fill vacancies on the Board. A majority vote of the current Directors will be required for election. Board-elected directors will serve until the next annual meeting, when a Board of Directors election will be held.

4.6 COMPENSATION.

Directors will serve voluntarily and will not receive compensation for their services except for expenses incurred and specified by Board resolutions. A Director may be compensated for services provided to the Corporation if he also serves in another position, such as an officer, agent, or employee.

Article 5---Officers

5.1 NUMBER OF OFFICERS.

The Corporation shall have at least a President and a Secretary. Other officers, along with titles and responsibilities, may be added by the Board of Directors. One person may be selected to serve in more than one position.

5.2 ELECTION.

The Board sets officers' election, length of term, and compensation.

5.3 REMOVAL AND RESIGNATION.

An officer may be removed or resign at any time, with or without cause. Removal requires an action of the Board. Resignation requires that the officer submit a written notice of his resignation to the Secretary.

5.4 PRESIDENT.

The President will serve, at the discretion and under the supervision of the Board, as the corporation's general manager and chief executive officer. The President will have the authority and power to run the company's day-to-day operations under the guidelines provided by the Board. Without a Treasurer, the President will also serve as the chief financial officer.

5.5 SECRETARY.

The Secretary will be responsible for:

(1) sending out notices for all meetings, (2) keeping minutes for all meetings, (3) maintaining the Corporate Record Book, (4) maintaining Corporation records and seal.

5.6 COMPENSATION.

The Board of Directors will set the compensation for officers. No officer will be denied compensation because they are also a Director.

Article 6---Authority to Execute

6.1 BINDING POWER.

No officer, agent, or any other person or company has the right or power to bind the Corporation by pledge, agreement, contract, or any other means without the expressed written permission of the Board of Directors.

6.2 SIGNATORIES.

With authorization from the Board of Directors, the President and Secretary will sign all documents, including all financial records requiring a corporate officer's signature or endorsement.

Article 7---Dissolution

Upon authorization from the Board of Directors to dissolve and after all liabilities of the Corporation have been addressed, the remaining assets of the Corporation maybe disposed of exclusively for the Corporation as the Board of Directors shall determine.

Article 8---Corporate Records

8.1 CORPORATE MINUTES.
A record of all meetings will be kept at the principal place of business or an alternate location chosen by the Board of Directors. The minutes shall include the date, time, location, names of attendees, purpose, and acts of each meeting.

8.2 FINANCIAL RECORDS.
The chief financial officer will maintain accurate records of all corporate financial transactions. Industry-acceptable accounting procedures are to be followed so that the records may be used to prepare the Corporation's tax returns.

8.3 INSPECTION OF RECORDS.
Corporate records and Bylaws are available for inspection by Directors. Before the examination, the inspecting party must sign an affidavit stating that the information will be confidential.

8.4 FISCAL YEAR.
The Board of Directors will determine the Corporation's fiscal year based on the prevailing guidelines of the Internal Revenue Service.

Article 9---Indemnification and Insurance

9.1 INDEMNIFICATION.

The Corporation will indemnify the directors and officers to the fullest extent of the law. Any director or officer found negligent or guilty of misconduct will forfeit their indemnification.

9.2 INSURANCE.

The Corporation shall have the power to purchase and maintain insurance for any agent of the Corporation, including but not limited to directors, officers, and employees

Article 10---Adoption

This is to certify that the foregoing is a true and correct copy of the Initial Bylaws duly adopted by the undersigned Board of Directors.

Date: _____, 20_____

Director _____

Director _____

Director _____

Secretary _____

www.ingramcontent.com/pod-product-compliance
Lightning Source LLC
Chambersburg PA
CBHW061703120626
46550CB00003B/1066